Black Book

Java™ 8
Exception
Handling
Quiz

Mahavir DS Rathore

<u>Books By Mahavir DS Rathore</u>

   a. **Java 8 Exception Handling**
   b. **Learn Java 8 in a Week**

Copyright

Java 8 Exception handling quiz is by Mahavir DS Rathore. While every precaution has been taken in the preparation of this book the author assume No responsibility for errors or omissions, or for damages resulting from the use of the information contained herein.

About the author

I have been programming and teaching Java for last 18 years. This book is an effort to document my knowledge to share with everyone across the world. I am available to do training on Java anywhere in the world. My email id is gurumahaveer@gmail.com.

Who should read the book?

This book is for programmers who already know Core Java (Java Standard Edition).

Acknowledgement

Java is owned by Oracle and trademark is acknowledged.

Dedication

To the inventors of the Java Language.

Feedback

Please share your feedback at gurumahaveer@gmail.com which will help me to improve this book.

Table of Content

Chapter 1
Software Setup

Q.1: What is the latest version of Java?	
A	7
B	6
C	9
D	8
	<----Right Answer

Q.2: JRE stands for	
A	Java Robust Engine
B	Java Required Engine
C	Java Runtime Engine
D	Java Runnable Engine
	<----Right Answer

Q. 3: JDK stands for	
A	Java Debugging Kit
B	Java Development Kit
C	Java Documentation Kit
D	Java Database Kit
	<----Right Answer

Q. 4: To compile and execute Java application .... is needed	
A	JDK
B	JRE
C	JME
D	JEE
	<----Right Answer

Q.5: Which environment variable (Windows OS) is set for accessing java compiler and java interpreter at command line?	
A	CLASSPATH
B	JAVAHOME
C	PATH

D	HOME
	<----Right Answer

Q.6: To just execute a Java application .... is needed at the minimum.

A	JME
B	JDK
C	JEE
D	JRE
	<----Right Answer

Q.7: The command for java interpreter (Windows OS) is ....

A	Javaip.exe
B	Javac.exe
C	Java.exe
D	Javai.exe
	<----Right Answer

Q.8: The command for Java compiler (Windows OS) is ....

A	Java.exe
B	Javacompiler.exe
C	Javacomp.exe
D	Javac.exe
	<----Right Answer

Q.9: In which folder is 32-bit JDK (Windows OS) is installed by default?

A	C:\Program Files\
B	C:\Windows\
C	C:\Java
D	C:\Program Files (x86)\
	<----Right Answer

Q.10: In which folder is 64-bit JDK (Windows OS) is installed by default?

A	C:\Program Files\
B	C:\Windows\
C	C:\Java
D	C:\Program Files (x86)\

	<----Right Answer

Answers:

Q.No	Ans	Explanation
1	D	The latest version of Java is version 8.
2	C	"JRE" stands for Java Runtime Engine.
3	B	"JDK" stands for Java Development Kit.
4	A	"JDK" is required for a Java program to be compiled and executed.
5	C	PATH environment variable contains the location of Java commands.
6	D	To just execute a java application only JRE is required.
7	C	"Java.exe" is the command to activate Java interpreter.
8	D	"Javac.exe" is the command to activate Java compiler.
9	D	32-bit application on Windows OS is installed in "C:\Program Files (x86)\ "folder by default.
10	A	64-bit application on Windows OS is installed in "C:\Program Files\" folder by default.

Chapter 2
What is an Exception?

Q.1: .... Occur at Runtime.	
A	Error
B	Exception
C	Trigger
D	None of the above
	<----Right Answer

Q.2: Runtime error is also called as	
A	Error
B	Compiler error
C	Exception
D	None of the above
	<----Right Answer

Q.3: Syntax error yields into a	
A	Runtime error
B	Exception
C	Compiler error
D	All of the above
	<----Right Answer

Q.4: Dividing an integer by zero yields into a	
A	Compiler error
B	JVM error
C	Nothing
D	Exception
	<----Right Answer

Q.5: A missing semi-colon for an instruction yields into a	
A	Exception
B	Runtime error
C	Compiler error
D	JVM error

<----Right Answer

Q.6: What will be the output?

```
class Program {
 public static void main(String args[]) {
  String ar = new String[1];
  ar[2] ="Ram";
  System.out.println(ar[0]);
 }
}
```

A	Compiler error
B	Exception
C	No error
D	JVM Load Failure
	<----Right Answer

Q.7: An exception can occur when ....

A	'throw' is called
B	Abnormal code is executed
C	Asynchronous error happen
D	All of the above
	<----Right Answer

Answers:

Q.No	Ans	Explanation
1	B	Exception occur at Runtime i.e. during program execution.
2	C	Another name for Runtime error is Exception.
3	C	Syntax error yields into a Compiler error.
4	D	Division by zero yields into ArithmeticException.
5	C	Missing semi-colon is captured as a Compiler error.
6	B	Exception "ArrayOutOfBounds" occur.
7	D	An exception can occur when any of below is called or occur a. 'throw' b. Abnormal code is executed c. Asynchronous error

Chapter 3
What is Exception Handling?

Q.1: .... helps in avoiding runtime crash of a program.	
A	Error handling
B	Exception handling
C	Compiler handling
D	Database handling
	<----Right Answer

Q.2: Which of the following is not a keyword?	
A	Throw
B	Throws
C	throwing
D	Try
	<----Right Answer

Q.3: Which of the following is not a keyword?	
A	try
B	catch
C	except
D	finally
	<----Right Answer

Q.4: How to raise an exception?	
A	throws
B	throw
C	except
D	raise
	<----Right Answer

Q.5: Who handles unhandled exceptions?	
A	JVM
B	OS
C	catch
D	finally

	<----Right Answer

Answers:

Q.No	Ans	Explanation
1	B	Exception handling is used for avoiding crash of a program.
2	C	'throwing' is not a keyword in Java.
3	C	'except' is not keyword in Java.
4	B	The 'throw' keyword is used for raising an exception.
5	A	JVM handles those exception that are not handled by a programmer which yields into an abnormal program termination.

Chapter 4
Java Exception Hierarchy

Q.1: .... class is the mother class of all exception classes (directly or indirectly).

A	Throwable
B	Exception
C	Error
D	Object
	<----**Right Answer**

Q.2: .... class is the mother class of "Exception" class.

A	Object
B	Error
C	Compiler
D	Throwable
	<----**Right Answer**

Q.3: .... is the mother class of "Error" class.

A	Object
B	Exception
C	Throwable
D	RuntimeException
	<----**Right Answer**

Q.4: .... is the mother class of "RuntimeException" class.

A	Error
B	Exception
C	Throwable
D	Object
	<----**Right Answer**

Q.5: Throwable class implements .... interface

A	Cloneable
B	Serializable
C	Runnable
D	Comparable

	<----Right Answer

Q.6: .... is the mother class of "Throwable" class.	
A	Object
B	Exception
C	Error
D	JVM
	<----Right Answer

Q.7: .... (And derived class) exception is not recoverable.	
A	Error class
B	Throwable class
C	Exception class
D	Object class
	<----Right Answer

Q.8: .... (And derived class) exception is asynchronous.	
A	Throwable class
B	Error class
C	Exception class
D	Object class
	<----Right Answer

Q.9: Which of the following is/are derived from "Error class"?	
A	StackoverflowError
B	OutOfMemoryError
C	VirtualMachineError
D	All of the above
	<----Right Answer

Q.10: When does ThreadDeath exception occur?	
A	Thread.abort()
B	Thread.stop()
C	Thread.exit()
D	Thread.quit()
	<----Right Answer

Q.11: Which exception occur when a method is called recursively?

A	OutOfMemoryError
B	OutOfMemoryException
C	StackoverflowException
D	StackoverflowError
	<----Right Answer

Q.12: .... (Exception) is compiler checked.

A	Error class
B	RuntimeException class
C	Exception class
D	Object class
	<----Right Answer

Q.13: .... (Exception) is not compiler checked.

A	Exception class
B	Throwable class
C	Object class
D	RuntimeException
	<----Right Answer

Q.14: Which of the following class is not derived from RuntimeException class?

A	NullPointerException
B	ArrayIndexOutOfBoundException
C	ArithmeticException
D	IOException
	<----Right Answer

Q.15: Which of following interfaces does Exception class implement?

A	Serializable
B	Throwable
C	Attribute
D	None of the above
	<----Right Answer

Q.16: Which of the following interfaces does Error class implement?

A	Serializable
B	Throwable
C	Atrribute
D	None of the above
	<----Right Answer

Q.17: .... exception is compiler checked.

A	Throwable class
B	Object class
C	Error class
D	RuntimeException class
	<----Right Answer

Answers:

Q.No	Ans	Explanation
1	A	Throwable class is the mother class of all exception classes (directly or indirectly).
2	D	Throwable class is the mother class of Exception.
3	C	Throwable class is the mother class of Error class.
4	B	Exception class is the mother class of Runtime class.
5	B	Serializable interface is implemented by Throwable class.
6	A	Object is the mother class of Throwable class.
7	A	Error class exception is not recoverable.
8	B	Error class exception is asynchronous.
9	D	StackoverflowError, OutOfMemoryError and VirtualMachineError classes are derived from Error class.
10	B	ThreadDeath Exception occurs when Thread.stop() is called.
11	D	StackoverflowError occur when a method is deeply recursive.
12	C	Exception class is identified by the compiler if not handled.
13	D	RuntimeException class is not identified by the compiler.
14	D	IOException derives from Exception class not RuntimeException.
15	D	Exception class does not implement any interface.
16	D	Error class does not implement any interface.
17	A	Throwable class exception is identified by compiler is not handled.

Chapter 5
Try and Catch Blocks

	Q.1: For an unhandled exception ....Is printed on the screen.
A	Call stack information
B	Assertion information
C	Debug information
D	None of the above
	<----Right Answer

	Q.2: Try block can be put inside a ....
A	Interface
B	Class
C	Method
D	Nested class
	<----Right Answer

	Q.3: An unhandled exception is handled by ....
A	Compiler
B	GC
C	JVM
D	None of the above
	<----Right Answer

	Q.4: Catch block only exists for a given ....
A	Code block
B	Try block
C	Data block
D	Nested block
	<----Right Answer

	Q.5: Try block cannot be put in a ....
A	Class
B	Interface
C	Constructor
D	Method

	<----Right Answer

Q.6: A static block can contain a try block.

A	TRUE
B	FALSE
	<----Right Answer

Q.7: A constructor can contain a try block.

A	TRUE
B	FALSE
	<----Right Answer

Answers:

Q.No	Ans	Explanation
1	A	Call stack (stacktrace) information is displayed on screen for an unhandled exception.
2	C	Try block can be put inside a method not anywhere else.
3	C	An unhandled exception is handled by JVM (which crashes an application).
4	B	Catch only exists for a try block.
5	A,B	Try block cannot be put in interface or a class.
6	A	A static block can contain a try block.
7	A	A constructor can contain a try block.

Chapter 6
Exception Handling API

Q.1: What is a call stack?	
A	Execution of main method.
B	Calling of a privileged method over regular method.
C	It is a stack data structure that store information about active methods.
D	Collection of functions.
	<----Right Answer

Q.2: .... method is used for printing call stack when an exception occur.	
A	callStack()
B	printStackTrace()
C	stackTrace()
D	stackInfo()
	<----Right Answer

Q.3: .... method is used for getting generic exception message.	
A	message()
B	toString()
C	getInfo()
D	msgException()
	<----Right Answer

Q.4: printStackTrace() method belong to .... class.	
A	Throwable
B	Error
C	Exception
D	Object
	<----Right Answer

Q.5: toString() method belong to .... class.	
A	Throwable
B	Error

C	Exception
D	Object
	<----Right Answer

Q.6: Return value of printStackTrace() method is ………………….	
A	String
B	char
C	void
D	char[]
	<----Right Answer

Answers:

Q.No	Ans	Explanation
1	C	Call stack is a stack data structure that store information about active methods.
2	B	printStackTrace() method is used for print call stack information when an exception occur.
3	B	toString() method returns generic exception information.
4	A	printStackTrace() method belong to Throwable class.
5	D	toString() method belong to Object class.
6	C	printStackTrace() method does not return anything.

Chapter 7
Multiple Catch

	Q.1: How many catch blocks can be added for a given try block?
A	1
B	2
C	15
D	Any Number
	<----Right Answer

	Q.2: In what order should the exceptions be caught using catch block?
A	In any order
B	In Top-Down order of inheritance hierarchy
C	In Bottom-Up order of inheritance hierarchy
D	Catch block does not handle exceptions
	<----Right Answer

	Q.3: What should be the order of catch blocks for the following exceptions? Throwable , Exception, RuntimeException
A	Any order
B	Throwable, Exception, RuntimeException
C	Exception,RuntimeException,Throwable
D	RuntimeException,Exception,Throwable
	<----Right Answer

	Q.4: 'try' block cannot encapsulate?
A	Code within method
B	Code within constructor
C	Code within static block
D	Class
	<----Right Answer

	Q.5: If exceptions are not handled in bottom-up order of inheritance hierarchy, What error do we encounter?

A	Compiler Error
B	Runtime Exception
C	Nothing happens
D	JVM Exception
	<----Right Answer

Answers:

Q.No	Ans	Explanation
1	D	A try block can have any number of catch blocks.
2	C	The catch block should catch exceptions in the bottom-up(reverse) order of inheritance hierarchy.
3	D	The correct order is RuntimException, Exception and Throwable class.
4	D	'Try' block cannot encapsulate a class.
5	A	If exception are not handled in the reverse order of their inheritance hierarchy compiler gives an error.

Chapter 8
Multiple Exceptions

Q.1: In which version of Java was this (Multiple exceptions in a single catch) capability added?	
A	6
B	5
C	7
D	8
	<----Right Answer

Q.2: What is the delimiter used to identify multiple exceptions in a single catch?	
A	| (pipe)
B	& (ampersand)
C	, (comma)
D	/(slash)
	<----Right Answer

Q.3: Identify the correct syntax	
A	catch(Error| Exception obj) {}
B	catch(Throwable | Exception) {}
C	catch(Throwable obj | Exception obj2) {}
D	Catch (...) {}
	<----Right Answer

Q.4: Mother and Child class exception cannot be caught in a single catch block.	
A	TRUE
B	FALSE
	<----Right Answer

Q.5: What happens when Mother and Child class exception is caught in a single catch block?	
A	No error or exception
B	Compiler Error

C	JVM Error
D	Runtime Exception
	<----Right Answer

Answers:

Q.No	Ans	Explanation
1	C	Multiple exception handling in a single catch was added in Java 7.
2	A	The delimiter used to segregate exceptions in a single catch is '|'.
3	A	Correct syntax is : catch(Error| Exception obj) {}
4	A	Mother and child class exception cannot be caught in a single catch.
5	B	Compiler gives an error when programmer tries to handle mother and class exception in a single catch.

Chapter 9
Finally Block

Q.1: How many 'finally' blocks can be added to 'try' block?	
A	1
B	2
C	3
D	Any number
	<----Right Answer

Q.2: The order of exception handling blocks (keywords) is	
A	try, finally, catch
B	catch,finally,try
C	try,catch,finally
D	Any order
	<----Right Answer

Q.3: 'finally' block does not execute when	
A	'return' keyword is called
B	Program exits
C	'finally' is guaranteed to be executed
D	None of the above
	<----Right Answer

Q.4: Identify the correct statement	
A	'Finally' block is compulsory for a given try.
B	'Finally' block is executed when an exception occurs.
C	'Finally' block is executed when there is no exception.
D	None of the above.
	<----Right Answer

Q.5: For a given 'try' block 'finally' block is placed after	
A	'try' block
B	'catch' block
C	'finally' block
D	Constructor

	<----Right Answer

Q.6: A try block requires at least .... Or ....

A	'catch' block
B	'finally' block
C	'try' block
D	Code block
	<----Right Answer

Q.7: If a 'try' block has both catch and finally blocks then .... will be placed first

A	'catch' block
B	'finally' block
C	Any order
D	None of the above
	<----Right Answer

Q.8: What will happen if a try block only has finally block and an exception occurs?

A	Program crashes
B	Program continues without crashes
C	The outcome is not predictable
D	Compiler error
	<----Right Answer

Answers:

Q.No	Ans	Explanation
1	A	Only one finally block can added for a given try block.
2	C	The order of exception handling blocks is – try, catch and finally.
3	B	'Finally' block is not executed when program exits.
4	B,C	'Finally' block is guaranteed to be executed with or without exception occurrence.
5	B	'Finally' block is placed after 'catch' block.
6	A,B	A 'try' block should have at least 'catch' or 'finally' block.
7	A	A 'try' block is followed by 'catch' block and then 'finally' block.
8	A	Program will crash if there is no catch block to handle the exception.

Chapter 10
Finally block & Return keyword

Q.1: How to abruptly stop an application execution?

A	System.stop()
B	System.abort()
C	System.kill()
D	System.exit()
	<----Right Answer

Q.2: 'finally' block is executed even if method encounter 'return' keyword.

A	TRUE
B	FALSE
	<----Right Answer

Q.3: 'finally' block is executed even if 'return' keyword is executed in 'catch' block.

A	TRUE
B	FALSE
	<----Right Answer

Q.4: 'finally' block is executed when a program execution is aborted.

A	TRUE
B	FALSE
	<----Right Answer

Q.5: 'finally' block is executed when a program encounters an exception in 'catch' block.

A	TRUE
B	FALSE
	<----Right Answer

Answers:

Q.No	Ans	Explanation
1	D	System.exit() is used to abruptly stop a program.
2	A	'Finally' block is executed even if program encounter 'return' keyword in method.
3	A	'Finally' block is executed even if program encounter 'return' keyword in catch block.
4	B	'Finally' block is not executed if program is aborted.
5	A	'Finally' block is executed even if exception happens in a catch block.

Chapter 11
Checked and Unchecked Exception

Q.1: .... exception is identified by the compiler	
A	Checked
B	Unchecked
C	Runtime
D	All of the above
	<----Right Answer

Q.2: .... exception is not identified by the compiler	
A	Unchecked
B	Checked
C	Compiler
D	JVM
	<----Right Answer

Q.3: .... exception has to be handled in a program.	
A	Compiler
B	Checked
C	Unchecked
D	JVM
	<----Right Answer

Q.4: .... exception need not be (compulsorily) handled in a program.	
A	Compiler
B	Checked
C	JVM
D	Unchecked
	<----Right Answer

Q.5: .... keyword is used for declaring an exception for a method.	
A	throw
B	throws
C	decl

D	finally
	<----Right Answer

Q.6: Checked exception can derive from ………… or …………… class

A	Throwable
B	Exception
C	Error
D	RuntimeException
	<----Right Answer

Q.7: How many exceptions can be declared using 'throws' keyword for a method?

A	1
B	2
C	3
D	Any number
	<----Right Answer

Q.8: Checked exception is verified by compiler.

A	TRUE
B	FALSE
	<----Right Answer

Q.9: Unchecked exception derive from ………… class

A	Throwable
B	Exception
C	Error
D	RuntimeException
	<----Right Answer

Q.10: Which of following is not an unchecked exception?

A	NullPointerException
B	ArithmeticException
C	ClassCastException
D	Exception
	<----Right Answer

Q.11: Which of following is not a checked exception?

A	NullPointerException
B	ArithmeticException
C	ClassCastException
D	Exception
	<----Right Answer

Answers:

Q.No	Ans	Explanation
1	A	Checked Exception is identified by the compiler.
2	A	Unchecked exception is not identified by the compiler.
3	B	Checked exception has to be handled (compulsory).
4	D	Unchecked exception is not required to be compulsorily handled.
5	B	'Throws' keyword is used for declaring an exception for a method.
6	A,B	Checked Exception can derive from Throwable or Exception class
7	D	Any number of exceptions can be declared using 'throws' keyword.
8	A	Checked exception is known at compile time.
9	D	Unchecked exceptions derive from RuntimeException class
10	D	Exception class is a checked exception.
11	A,B, C	NullPointerException, ArithmeticException and ClassCastException are not checked exceptions.

Chapter 12
Nested Exception

Q.1: Java has support for nested exception handling.	
A	TRUE
B	FALSE
	<----Right Answer

Q.2: Upto what level of nesting of exception handling does Java support?	
A	1
B	2
C	3
D	Any Level
	<----Right Answer

Q.3: What is the output?

```
class Program {
 static void performJob() {
  try {
    int j = 10/0;
  }catch(ArrayIndexOutOfBoundsException e) {
    System.out.println("Handle the array carefully");
  }
 }
 public static void main(String args[]) {
  try {
    performJob();
  } catch (Exception e) {
    System.out.println("There is some problem in the code");
  }
 }
}
```

A	No output
B	Handle the array carefully
C	There is some problem in the code
D	Division by zero
	<----Right Answer

Q.4: What is the output?

```
class Program {
 static void performJob() {
  try {
    int j = 10/0;
  }catch(ArrayIndexOutOfBoundsException e) {
   System.out.println("Handle the array carefully");
  }
  finally {
        System.out.println("finally - performJob");
  }
 }
 public static void main(String args[]) {
  try {
    performJob();
  } catch (Exception e) {
   System.out.println("There is some problem in the code");
  }
  finally {
        System.out.println("finally - main");
  }
 }
}
```

A	No output
B	finally - performJob
	There is some problem in the code
	finally – main
C	finally - performJob
	finally – main
D	There is some problem in the code
	finally – main
	finally - performJob
	<----Right Answer

Q.5: What is the output?

```
class Program {
 static void performJob() {
  try {
    int j = 10/0;
  }catch(ArrayIndexOutOfBoundsException e) {
   System.out.println("Handle the array carefully");
  }
  finally {
        System.out.println("finally - performJob");
  }
 }
 public static void main(String args[]) {
```

```
          int ar[] = new int[1];
    try {
            ar[1]=0;
      performJob();
    } catch (Exception e) {
      System.out.println("There is some problem in the code");
    }
    finally {
            System.out.println("finally - main");
    }
  }
}
```

A	No output
B	There is some problem in the code finally – main
C	finally - performJob There is some problem in the code finally – main
D	finally - performJob There is some problem in the code
	<----Right Answer

Answers:

Q.No	Ans	Explanation
1	A	Java has support for exception handling
2	D	Java exception can be nested upto any level.
3	C	By computation the output is : There is some problem in the code
4	B	By computation the output is: finally - performJob There is some problem in the code finally - main
5	B	By computation the output is : There is some problem in the code finally - main

Chapter 13
'Throw' Keyword

Q.1: Class derived from .... can only be thrown.	
A	Object
B	Throwable
C	GC
D	All of the above
	<----Right Answer

Q.2: .... Keyword is used to raise an exception.	
A	throw
B	throws
C	raise
D	signal
	<----Right Answer

Q.3: What is the output?

```
class Program {
 public static void main(String args[]) {
  try {
     throw new Exception();
  } catch (Exception e) {
    System.out.println("There is some problem in the code");
  }
  finally {
       System.out.println("finally - main");
  }
 }
}
```

A	No output
B	There is some problem in the code
C	There is some problem in the code finally – main
D	finally – main
	<----Right Answer

Q.4: What is output?

```
class Program {
 static void performJob() {
```

```
    try {
      throw new ArrayIndexOutOfBoundsException();
    }catch(ArrayIndexOutOfBoundsException e) {
      System.out.println("Handle the array carefully");
    }
    finally {
        System.out.println("finally - performJob");
    }
  }
}
 public static void main(String args[]) {
   try {
     performJob();
   } catch (Exception e) {
     System.out.println("There is some problem in the code");
   }
   finally {
        System.out.println("finally - main");
   }
  }
}
}
```

A	finally - performJob finally – main
B	No output
C	Handle the array carefully finally - performJob
D	Handle the array carefully finally - performJob finally - main
	<----Right Answer

Q.5: What is the output?

```
class Program {
 static void performJob() {
  try {
    throw new ArrayIndexOutOfBoundsException();
  }catch(ArrayIndexOutOfBoundsException e) {
        throw new Exception();
    System.out.println("Handle the array carefully");
  }
  finally {
        System.out.println("finally - performJob");
  }
 }
 public static void main(String args[]) {
  try {
    performJob();
```

```
  } catch (Exception e) {
    System.out.println("There is some problem in the code");
  }
  finally {
      System.out.println("finally - main");
  }
 }
}
```

A	No output
B	Compiler Error
C	Handle the array carefully finally - performJob finally - main
D	finally - performJob finally - main
	<----Right Answer

Q.6: What is the output?

```
class Program {
 static void performJob() {
  try {
    throw new ArrayIndexOutOfBoundsException();
  }
catch(ArrayIndexOutOfBoundsException e) {
        throw new Exception();
    System.out.println("Handle the array carefully");
  }
  finally {
        System.out.println("finally - performJob");
  }
 }
 public static void main(String args[]) {
  try {
    performJob();
  } catch (Exception e) {
    System.out.println("There is some problem in the code");
  }
  finally {
        System.out.println("finally - main");
  }
 }
}class Program {
 static void performJob() {
  try {
    throw new ArrayIndexOutOfBoundsException();
  }catch(ArrayIndexOutOfBoundsException e) {
```

```
        try {
        throw new Exception();
        }catch(Exception obj) {
                System.out.println("This is inner exception");
        }
    System.out.println("Handle the array carefully");
    }
    finally {
        System.out.println("finally - performJob");
    }
}
public static void main(String args[]) {
    try {
        performJob();
    } catch (Exception e) {
        System.out.println("There is some problem in the code");
    }
    finally {
        System.out.println("finally - main");
    }
  }
}
```

A	No output
B	Compiler Error
C	This is inner exception finally - performJob finally - main
D	This is inner exception Handle the array carefully finally - performJob finally - main
	<----Right Answer

Answers:

Q.No	Ans	Explanation
1	B	Class derived from 'Throwable'(or derived class) can only be thrown
2	A	'throw' keyword is used for raising an exception.
3	C	By computation the output is: There is some problem in the code finally - main

4	D	By computation the output is : Handle the array carefully finally - performJob finally - main
5	B	Compiler Error
6	D	By Computation the output is. This is inner exception Handle the array carefully finally - performJob finally - main

Chapter 14
Exception Chaining

Q.1: .... class has infrastructure support for exception chaining.	
A	Exception
B	Throwable
C	Error
D	RuntimeException
	<----Right Answer

Q.2: getCause() method is declared in .... class	
A	Object
B	Error
C	RuntimeException
D	Throwable
	<----Right Answer

Q.3: Identify the correct constructor for 'Throwable' class.	
A	Throwable(String, Throwable)
B	Throwable(String[], Throwable)
C	Throwable(char[], Throwable)
D	Throwable(char, Throwable)
	<----Right Answer

Q.4: Which method initializes the cause of an exception?	
A	start Cause()
B	setCause()
C	setIssue()
D	initCause()
	<----Right Answer

Q.5: Identify the correct constructor for 'Throwable' class.	
A	Throwable(int)
B	Throwable(String[])

C	Throwable(Throwable)
D	Throwable()
	<----Right Answer

Q.6: initCause() method is declared in .... class

A	Object
B	Throwable
C	RuntimeException
D	Error
	<----Right Answer

Q.7: .... method return the cause of a 'throwable'.

A	getMsg()
B	getMessage()
C	getCause()
D	getReason()
	<----Right Answer

Answers:

Q.No	Ans	Explanation
1	B	Throwable class has infrastructure for exception chaining.
2	D	getCause() method is declared in Throwable class.
3	A	Valid constructor is : Throwable(String, Throwable)
4	D	initCause() method initializes the cause of an exception.
5	C,D	Valid constructors are : Throwable(Throwable) Throwable()
6	B	initCause() method is declared in Throwable class.
7	C	getCause() method return the cause of a 'throwable'.

Chapter 15
Try with Resource

Q.1: In which version of Java was 'try with resource' introduced?	
A	5
B	6
C	7
D	8
	<----Right Answer

Q.2: How many resources can be created in a single try block?	
A	None
B	2
C	3
D	Any
	<----Right Answer

Q.3: An object has to implement .... or .... to be eligible in "try with resource" block.	
A	AutoCloseable
B	Closeable
C	TryClose
D	Closed
	<----Right Answer

Q.4: Identify the method of AutoCloseable interface?	
A	Close()
B	close()
C	Closing
D	Closed
	<----Right Answer

Q.5: Identify the method of Closeable interface?	
A	closed()
B	closing()
C	close()
D	end()

	<----Right Answer

Q.6: The resources are closed in .... order when created in 'try with resource'.

A	Custom
B	Forward
C	Reverse
D	Conditional
	<----Right Answer

Q.7: What is the output

```java
import java.io.*;

class Shape implements Closeable {
    public void close() {
        System.out.println("Shape object close is closed");
    }
}
class Program {
    public static void main(String args[]){
        try(Shape obj = new Shape()) {

        }catch(Exception e) {
            System.out.println("Exception happened");
        }
    }
}
```

A	No Output
B	Compiler Error
C	Shape object close is closed
D	Exception happened
	<----Right Answer

Answers:

Q.No	Ans	Explanation
1	C	'Try with resource' was introduced in Java 7.
2	D	Any number of resources can be created in a try.
3	A,B	An object is only eligible in try with resource when it implements Closeable or AutoCloseable.

4	B	AutoCloseable has only one method i.e. close()
5	C	Closeable interface has only one method i.e. close().
6	C	The objects are closed in the reverse order of declaration.
7	C	The output is : Shape object close is closed

Chapter 16
Overriding Exception

Q.1: What is the output?

```
class Shape {
 void draw () {
  System.out.println("Drawing shape");
 }
}

class Circle extends Shape{
  void draw() throws RuntimeException {
    System.out.println("Drawing Circle");
  }
}

class Program {
public static void main(String args[]) {
          Circle obj = new Circle();
          obj.draw();
      }
}
```

A	Compiler error
B	No output
C	Drawing shape
D	Drawing Circle
	<----Right Answer

Q.2: What is the output?

```
class Shape {
 void draw () {
  System.out.println("Drawing shape");
 }
}

class Circle extends Shape{
  void draw() throws Exception {
    System.out.println("Drawing Circle");
  }
}
```

```
class Program {
 public static void main(String args[]) {
            Circle obj = new Circle();
            obj.draw();
      }
}
```

A	Compiler error
B	No output
C	Drawing shape
D	Drawing Circle
	<----Right Answer

Q.3: What is the output?

```
class Shape {
 void draw () throws Exception {
  System.out.println("Drawing shape");
 }
}

class Circle extends Shape{
  void draw() throws Throwable {
     System.out.println("Drawing Circle");
   }
}

class Program {
 public static void main(String args[]) throws Exception{
            Circle obj = new Circle();
            obj.draw();
      }
}
```

A	Compiler error
B	No output
C	Drawing shape
D	Drawing Circle
	<----Right Answer

Q.4: What is the output?

```
class Shape {
 void draw () throws Exception {
  System.out.println ("Drawing shape");
 }
}
```

```
class Circle extends Shape{
 void draw() throws Exception {
   System.out.println("Drawing Circle");
  }
}

class Program {
        public static void main(String args[]) throws Exception{
                Circle obj = new Circle();
                obj.draw();
        }
}
```

A	Compiler error
B	No output
C	Drawing shape
D	Drawing Circle
	<----Right Answer

Q.5: What is the output?

```
class Shape {
 void draw () throws Exception {
   System.out.println("Drawing shape");
 }
}
class Circle extends Shape{
void draw() throws RuntimeException {
   System.out.println("Drawing Circle");
  }
}
class Program {
        public static void main(String args[]) throws Exception{
                Circle obj = new Circle();
                obj.draw();
        }
}
```

A	Compiler error
B	No output
C	Drawing shape
D	Drawing Circle
	<----Right Answer

Rules for exceptions in overridden methods:

a. If the super class method 'throws' an exception then child class can 'throws' the same exception or child class of that exception.

b. If super class method does not 'throws' any exception then the child class overridden method can 'throws' unchecked exception.

c. If checked exception is declared for a method then it should be raised (throw).

Answers:

Q.No	Ans	Explanation
1	D	By computation the output is : Drawing Circle
2	A	Compiler Error
3	A	Compiler Error
4	D	By computation the output is : Drawing Circle
5	D	By computation the output is : Drawing Circle

Chapter 17
User Defined Exception

Q.1: How to create user defined checked exception?	
A	Derive from Error class
B	Derive from Throwable class
C	Derive from RuntimeException class
D	Derive from Object class
	<----Right Answer

Q.2: How to create user defined unchecked exception?	
A	Derive from Error class
B	Derive from Exception class
C	Derive from RuntimeException class
D	Derive from Object class
	<----Right Answer

Q.3: What is the output?

```
class MyException extends Object {
      MyExcetion(String str) {
            super(str);
      }
}

class Program {
      public static void main(String args[]){
            int i=10;
            int j=11;
            if (j> i)
            throw new MyException("j is greater");
      }
}
```

A	Compiler Error
B	Runtime Exception
C	J is greater
D	None of the above
	<----Right Answer

Q.4: What is the output?

```
class MyException extends Exception {
      MyException(String str) {
             super(str);
      }
}

class Program {
      public static void main(String args[]){
             int i=10;
             int j=11;
             if (j> i)
                    throw new MyException("j is greater");
      }
}
```

A	Compiler Error
B	Runtime Exception
C	J is greater
D	None of the above
	<----Right Answer

Q.5: What is the output?

```
class MyException extends RuntimeException {
      MyException(String str) {
             super(str);
      }
}

class Program {
      public static void main(String args[]){
             int i=10;
             int j=11;
             if (j> i)
             throw new MyException("j is greater");
      }
}
```

A	RuntimeException
B	Compiler Error
C	JVM Error
D	None of the above
	<----Right Answer

Q.6: What is the output?

```
class MyException extends Exception {
      MyException(String str) {
             super(str);
```

```
        }
}

class Program {
        public static void main(String args[]) throws Exception{
                int i=10;
                int j=11;
                if (j> i)
                throw new MyException("j is greater");
        }
}
```

A	Object Exception
B	JVM Error
C	Runtime Exception
D	Compiler Error
	<----Right Answer

Answers:

Q.No	Ans	Explanation
1	B	User defined checked exception is created by deriving from Throwable class.
2	C	User defined unchecked exception is created by deriving from RuntimeException class.
3	A	By computation the output is : Compiler Error
4	A	By computation the output is : Compiler Error
5	A	By computation the output is : Runtime Exception
6	C	By computation the output is : Runtime Exception

www.ingramcontent.com/pod-product-compliance
Lightning Source LLC
Chambersburg PA
CBHW060507060326
40689CB00020B/4670